MEDICINAL PLANTS
Coloring Book

ILIL ARBEL

Dover Publications, Inc.
New York

Copyright

Bibliographical Note

Medicinal Plants Coloring Book is a new work, first published by Dover Publications, Inc., in 1992.

DOVER *Pictorial Archive* SERIES

International Standard Book Number
ISBN-13: 978-0-486-27462-1
ISBN-10: 0-486-27462-4

Manufactured in the United States by Courier Corporation
27462409
www.doverpublications.com

Publisher's Note

With the recent widespread destruction of tropical rain forests has come an anguished outcry for their preservation. Not the least important reason is that so many plants of medicinal value, actual or potential, grow there. For millennia, early and "primitive" cultures have understood the healing and restorative properties of wild plants, and not only those growing in rain forests or the tropics. Even with the modern ability to synthesize drugs, wild plants are today of crucial importance in pharmacology. Without substances extracted from wild plants, so many troublesome, even fatal, conditions would still be medically untreatable. A vast uncharted region remains for continued research into new medicinal substances from the vegetable world, promising new treatments hitherto undreamt of.

For the present selection, artist Ilil Arbel has drawn, in a manner suitable for coloring, forty-four plants from all over the globe that are known for their past or present medicinal value. On many of them also rests the hope of outstanding pharmaceutical discoveries of the future.

All forty-four drawings are reproduced in color on the covers. The plants are arranged alphabetically by common name; alphabetical lists of scientific and common names (including a few alternate names) appear on the last page of the book.

NOTE: The captions in this book are strictly for informational purposes. No recommendation as to the actual medicinal use of any plant is intended. Many plants and substances derived from them are highly toxic, and dangerous when used improperly. The use of some is illegal. Individual captions to the drawings include warnings where appropriate. It must be realized, however, that harm may be caused by the ingestion or application of incorrect doses of otherwise harmless substances. No plant illustrated in this book should be used except according to the advice or under the supervision of a properly trained professional.

Aconite (*Aconitum napellus*). Aconite, also called monkshood (among many other names), is native to the mountains of northern Europe. This perennial grows up to three feet and has light green foliage and blue-purple flowers. White forms also exist. The plant yields aconitine, formerly used in the treatment of neuralgia and rheumatism. Aconite is extremely poisonous yet was used as a medicinal for centuries. Nowadays less toxic substances are usually substituted. In the middle ages it was a major ingredient in witches' brew! (*Poison.*)

"Aloe vera" *(Aloe barbadensis).* A perennial, one to two feet high, native to islands off the coast of north Africa, and frequently cultivated in the Netherlands Antilles, this is the plant, one of many aloes, most commonly known as "Aloe vera," a name without true scientific standing. The thick leaves are light green, mottled with white on younger plants. Flowers are yellow to purple. Leaves that are cut and left to drip yield glycosidal juice; crushed leaves yield a gel. Both are used to treat burns, especially X-ray burns, as well as various other skin conditions.

Arnica *(Arnica montana)*. This native of Europe, found mostly in the Alps, is a perennial that grows to two feet. The leaves are olive-green and the flowers golden-yellow. The plant yields arnicin, arnisterol, anthoxanine and tan-nin. The flowers and roots are used to produce a liniment for treating bruises and sprains. Arnica has also been used experimentally to treat salmonella and reduce fevers.

Balm-of-Gilead *(Populus balsamifera)*. A full-sized tree, growing to ninety feet, native to northeastern North America. Leaves are dark above, almost white underneath; flowers grow in red-white catkins. The fragrant, yellowish leaf buds yield glycosides, including salicin and populin. Used to treat chest infections, rheumatism and sore throat, and as a pain killer.

Belladonna *(Atropa belladonna)*. Belladonna, or deadly nightshade, is a European perennial growing most commonly to three feet, with dull green foliage, brownish purple flowers and shiny black berries. Known since antiquity, it is illustrated in all the great herbals and was widely used in witchcraft and alchemy. The alkaloid atropine, made from the roots, although a deadly poison, has had extremely diverse applications, even as an *antidote* to poisoning. It dilates the pupils of the eyes, an effect once exploited for its cosmetic value (hence the name *belladonna*, Italian for "beautiful lady"); more recently it has had essential uses in ophthalmology. It is a diuretic, it relieves respiratory congestion, and its powerful antispasmodic properties have been used to treat palsy, cardiac palpitations, intestinal spasms and asthma. *(Poison.)*

Hedge Bindweed (*Calystegia sepium*). This native of Europe and Asia has become widespread in the United States. It is a trailing perennial vine with a creeping rootstock and white or pink flowers like those of the morning glory, to which it is related. The root is used as a purgative, as a cure for jaundice, for ailments of the gall bladder and to increase the flow of bile into the intestines.

Boneset (*Eupatorium perfoliatum*). This North American perennial grows to four feet, its flowers ranging in color from white to pale purple. For generations boneset has been used to treat colds, flu and rheumatism. Recent research supports its value as an immune-system stimulant. It yields the glycoside eupatorine, which relieves the symptoms of the common cold. It also yields flavones and lactones that are being investigated in Europe for their possible anticancer effect. (Large doses may be *poisonous*.)

Great Burdock *(Arctium lappa)*. This native of Europe and Asia, now also spread across North America, is a biennial that grows to nine feet. The leaves are grayish beneath, and the flowers are reddish purple. The dried roots and seeds yield inulin and some antibiotic substances. The plant is used as a diuretic and laxative, and for the treatment of skin conditions like eczema and psoriasis. Burdock is also effective against rheumatism and gout, encouraging the elimination of uric acid via the kidneys. Studies made in Japan show that some of its compounds curb mutation, which suggests that someday the plant may be successfully used to treat cancer. (Leaves may *irritate skin*.)

Castor Bean *(Ricinus communis)*. This native of Africa, also called the castor-oil-plant, is now found everywhere. In temperate regions it is an annual that grows to twelve feet, but in the tropics it is a perennial that reaches over thirty feet. Its foliage is dark and glossy, its flowers red or white. The poisonous seeds are black, sometimes mottled with gray or brown. The oil extracted from them (leaving behind the poison) is well known as a purgative; it is also used as a base for eye ointments and in emollients such as zinc-and-castor-oil cream. Castor oil has also been applied as a medicine for ringworm and an ingredient in soap, among other uses. (Seeds *poisonous*.)

Chamomile *(Chamaemelum nobile).* This is one of the best-known medicinal plants, having been used since ancient times. A native of southern Europe, chamomile is a perennial, growing a foot high from a creeping rootstock. The flowers are white with yellow centers, the root brown.

An infusion of the dried flowers is used as a sedative, for relieving insomnia and nervousness and for treating digestive problems. The very similar German chamomile *(Chamaemelum recutita)* has the same uses.

Chicory *(Cichorium intybus)*. This lovely native of the Mediterranean may now be found growing wild throughout much of North America. A tall perennial, growing up to five feet, it has gray-green foliage and stemless sky-blue flowers (pink and white forms also exist). Its roots are a well-known coffee substitute, its leaves used as salad greens. Less well known are chicory's many medicinal uses. Yielding inulin and cichoroium, it is used to increase the flow of bile and as a remedy for gallstones and infections. Chicory eliminates uric acid from the body and is thus effective against rheumatism and gout. It is currently being tested on animals for the treatment of rapid heartbeat.

Coca *(Erythroxylum coca)*. Coca, or the cocaine plant, is a shrub growing to twelve feet, with white flowers and red or reddish brown berries. Originating in the Andes, it is now also cultivated elsewhere, particularly southeast Asia. Traditionally, Andean natives who chewed the leaves could labor for days without rest or nourishment. The alkaloid cocaine, a fine white powder extracted from these leaves, was once important in medicine as a local anesthetic. It has a powerful effect on the nervous system, the smoking, sniffing or injecting of it producing highly stimulating and euphoric effects. Addictive in prolonged use, in large doses it is toxic, even deadly. Widespread use of cocaine has led to serious social problems, and its use is illegal in many places. *(Poison.)*

Comfrey *(Symphytum officinale)*. This native of Europe and Asia is a thick-rooted perennial growing up to three feet. The leaves are lighter below than above, the root is brownish black, and the flowers are purple-blue, pink or white. Comfrey yields allantoin, which by promoting cell proliferation encourages the growth of connective tissue, bone and cartilage. It also breaks down red blood cells, which helps the healing of bruises and various ulcers.

Cornflower *(Centaurea cyanus)*. This annual, a native of Europe and the Near East, grows to two feet with gray-green foliage and flowers of an extremely intense blue (there are also pink and white forms). The plant yields cyanine and some sterols and has been used successfully as an eyewash for conjunctivitis and an ingredient in cough mixtures.

17

Dandelion (*Taraxacum officinale*). This familiar perennial "weed" with dark foliage and bright yellow flowers is a native of Europe and Asia but found all over. The dandelion is one of the best-known medicinal plants. A tea made from the roots is a well-known diuretic; with its excess potassium, it is safer than many drugs that tend to leach potassium out of the body. Dandelions yield taraxacin, which, stimulating the liver and gall bladder, increases the flow of bile and is a tonic for impaired digestion. Currently under way are experiments using the dandelion against yeast infection and as a weight-loss agent.

Dayflower (*Commelina communis*). This perennial, growing to three feet, is a native of Asia but widespread in the United States. Its foliage is bright green, its flowers blue, with one small white petal underneath. For many years a tea made from the leaves has been used as a gargle for sore throats, as a diuretic that is particularly effective when flu is present, and for tonsillitis, urinary infections and dysentery.

19

Elecampane (*Inula helenium*). A native of Europe and Asia, this perennial grows to eight feet. The leaves are olive-green with white veins, the root is brown, and the flowers are yellow. The plant is a source of the carbohydrate inulin and various volatile oils. It is an antibacterial, and is also used as a remedy for lung ailments and for various skin problems. In experiments on mice it has proved a strong sedative, and in China it has been used experimentally against certain cancers.

Evening Primrose *(Oenothera biennis)*. This biennial, native to North America but widely introduced in Europe as well, grows to six feet; its flowers are bright yellow. It is interesting to note that this plant was not used extensively in the past. Yet the current uses of the evening primrose are numerous and important: it is a source of gamma-linolenic acid, a balancing agent for abnormalities of essential fatty acids in prostaglandin production, an aid to estrogen production (menopause symptoms are greatly alleviated by evening primrose oil), a remedy for skin problems, dried-eye syndrome and (when combined with fish oil) rheumatoid arthritis, and a calming agent for hyperactive children.

Foxglove (*Digitalis purpurea*). This biennial or perennial grows to five feet; it is a native of southern Europe, now also common in New England. The foliage is gray underneath, the flowers rose-purple on the outside, white with red spots on the inside. Digitalis, now usually prepared from the dried, finely powdered leaves, contains valuable glycosides that have long been essential in heart medicine. In association with its stimulation of the heart and influencing the circulation of the blood, digitalis acts as a diuretic. (*Poison.*)

Yellow Gentian *(Gentiana lutea)*. This perennial, a native of central and southern Europe, grows up to six feet. It has a thick taproot, bright yellow-green foliage and bright yellow flowers. The dried roots and rhizome yield various glycosides, including amarogentine, one of the bitterest substances known. Gentian has often been used as a tonic to improve the appetite by promoting the flow of digestive juices and bile. Gentianin, an alkaloid, is anti-inflammatory.

American Ginseng *(Panax quinquefolius).* Native to the eastern and midwestern United States, American ginseng is a perennial growing to two feet. It has a fleshy root, white flowers and red berries. Long considered a cure-all in China, where it is still imported from America, its value has been strongly supported by recent research. American ginseng enhances mental and physical performance with its "adaptogenic" effect, restoring normal functioning after periods of stress or exposure to excessively high or low temperatures. Its valuable constituents include vitamins, minerals and hormone-like saponins. (Large doses may be mildly *poisonous*.)

Jewelweed *(Impatiens capensis).* Native to much of North America, jewelweed is an annual growing to five feet, with pale green foliage and orange flowers with red spots. Well known for its value in treating skin problems, the crushed leaves and stem juice of jewelweed are used for insect bites, eczema and other conditions. A particularly valuable use is in relieving the effects of poison-ivy rash.

Jimson Weed *(Datura stramonium)*. Jimson weed, or thorn apple, is probably native to the Americas but is so well distributed worldwide that its origin has been disputed. A perennial growing to five feet, it has flowers ranging from white to violet, sometimes on the same plant. As the plant matures, the seed capsules turn from dark green to golden brown, and the seeds to dark brown.

Like belladonna, to which it is related, the plant contains atropine and other alkaloids, and has been used for medical, magical and narcotic purposes since antiquity. Besides its uses in treating asthma, Parkinson's disease and eye diseases, the scopolamine it yields is used in patches placed behind the ears to control vertigo. *(Poison.)*

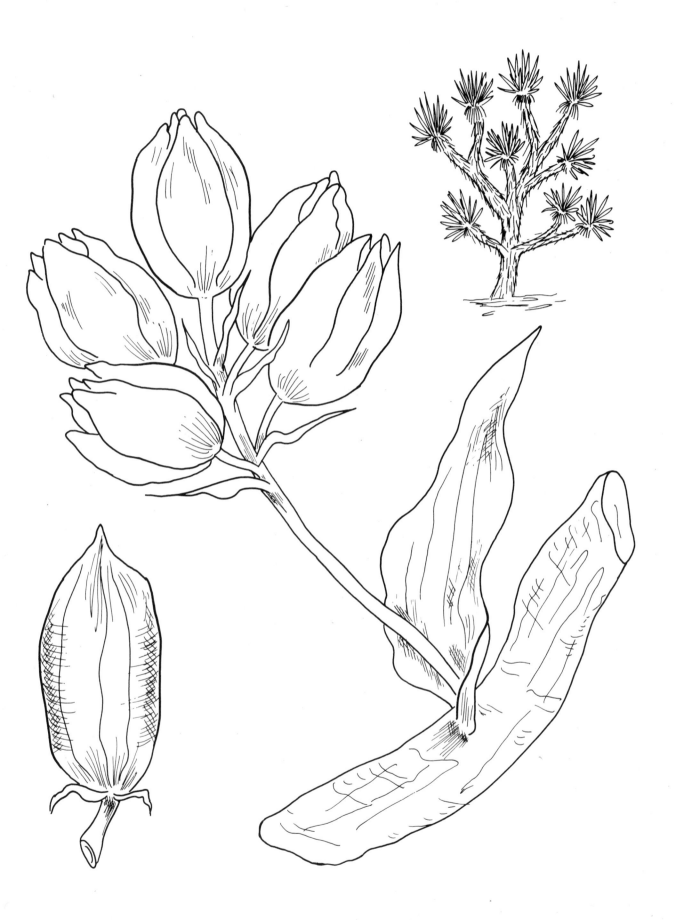

Joshua Tree *(Yucca brevifolia)*. This yucca, native to the southwestern United States, is a full-sized evergreen tree, growing to forty feet. The bark is dark brown, the flowers greenish white to greenish yellow. The seed pods are at first tan or light red, deepening to dark brown with age. From the Joshua tree come steroidal sapogenins, used to produce cortisone and estrogenic hormones.

Lavender (*Lavandula angustifolia*). This small shrub is native to the mountainous regions of the Mediterranean but cultivated extensively elsewhere, especially England. It grows up to three feet and has gray-green foliage and gray-blue flowers. Lavender was used as a perfume as far back as antiquity and for hundreds of years as a flavoring agent as well. Its volatile oil has medicinal properties; it has been used to treat burns, stings, headaches, coughs, colds and various nervous disorders.

Lily-of-the-Valley (*Convallaria majalis*). This native of Europe is also widespread elsewhere. A perennial that grows to eight inches, it has dark foliage and flower stalks that each bear a number of white, bell-like flowers. The fruits are bright red berries. Lily-of-the-valley yields valuable glycosides, one of which, a substitute for digitalis, is used to treat heart disease. The plant also has diuretic properties. In Russia it is used to treat epilepsy. (*Poison.*)

Lobelia *(Lobelia inflata)*. This two-foot-high annual is native to North America. The small flowers are white or pale blue. There are also small, green inflated seed pods. The dried foliage, which was smoked by American Indians, yields fourteen different alkaloids. Lobeline sulfate is used to treat respiratory ailments and in antismoking pills, and is an antispasmodic and emetic as well. Isobeline is a respiratory relaxant. Liniments made from lobelia are used to treat bruises and muscle spasms. *(Poison.)*

Mandrake *(Mandragora officinarum)*. This Mediterranean perennial grows to about a foot. It has a thick, tuberous root, dark foliage, greenish yellow or purplish flowers and orange fruit. Since ancient times, mandrake, a member of the nightshade family, has been associated with magic and witchcraft, and its humanlike form when uprooted has been the source of much folklore. It was also one of the first herbs used as a sedative and anesthetic in medicine. The root yields several alkaloids, including podophyllin, hyoscyamine and mandragorin. *(Poison.)*

Marigold (*Tagetes patula*). A bushy annual, growing to a foot and a half, this popular garden ornamental comes from Mexico and Guatemala (related species are from other parts of North and South America; European marigolds are more distantly related). It is familiar for its bright yellow or orange flowers, marked with brown or reddish brown. The foliage is olive green. Marigolds are covered with glands containing aromatic oils, esters and phenols, used to make analgesics, antiseptics and stimulants.

Marijuana *(Cannabis sativa)*. This annual is a native of Asia, though now found throughout the world, often as a weed. It has dark foliage and greenish flowers and grows to fourteen feet. Although illegal in the United States because of the dried leaves' intoxicating properties when smoked, marijuana has been found to have considerable medicinal value. Among its various uses, it is an antibiotic for gram-positive bacteria, relieves nausea induced by chemotherapy and has been used to treat glaucoma.

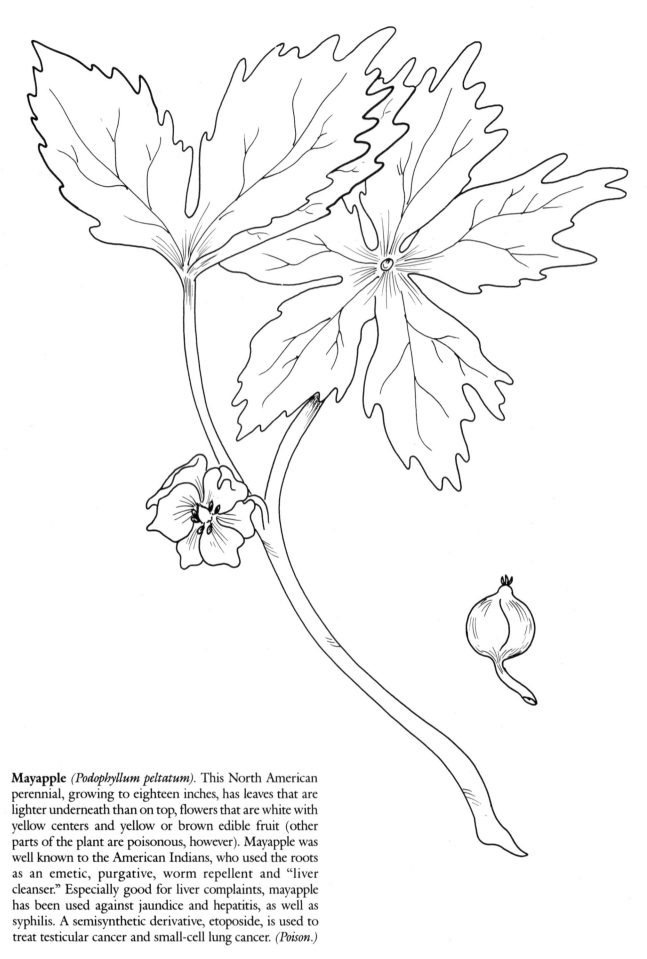

Mayapple (*Podophyllum peltatum*). This North American perennial, growing to eighteen inches, has leaves that are lighter underneath than on top, flowers that are white with yellow centers and yellow or brown edible fruit (other parts of the plant are poisonous, however). Mayapple was well known to the American Indians, who used the roots as an emetic, purgative, worm repellent and "liver cleanser." Especially good for liver complaints, mayapple has been used against jaundice and hepatitis, as well as syphilis. A semisynthetic derivative, etoposide, is used to treat testicular cancer and small-cell lung cancer. (*Poison.*)

34

Opium Poppy *(Papaver somniferum)*. This native of western Asia and southeastern Europe is an annual that grows to four feet; it bears white, pink, red or purple flowers with yellow centers. Valued as an ornamental, this poppy is much better known, of course, as the source of opium, derived from the milky sap of the unripe green seed capsule. The first use of opium is lost in antiquity; its medicinal properties, however, have been known for thousands of years. A number of its many alkaloids, including morphine and codeine, have been chemically extracted for over a century and a half for their important medical use as narcotics, analgesics, sedatives and antispasmodics (as in cough medicine). Addiction to opium first became a widespread social problem in seventeenth-century China, as that to the morphine derivative called heroin is in the United States today. *(Poison.)*

Passionflower (*Passiflora incarnata*). This passionflower, native to the southeast and south-central United States, is one of a large group of hundreds of plants found mostly in tropical America. *Passiflora incarnata* is a vine that can climb to thirty feet, with lovely white to purplish flowers bearing odd-looking filaments radiating from the center; its bright yellow fruits are edible, though mildly toxic in large quantities. Traditionally this passionflower, or may-pop, has been valued for its sedative properties and used as a remedy for insomnia, neuralgia, even epilepsy. Extracts of the plant have been demonstrated to decrease motor activity and blood pressure and slightly increase the respiratory rate. (Mildly *poisonous*.)

Pomegranate *(Punica granatum).* This small tree (growing to twenty feet) from the Middle East has been valued for thousands of years for its edible brownish red fruit. Its flowers are orange-red. The rind, a powerful astringent, has been used against dysentery and severe diarrhea. The antibacterial properties of the leaves have been used by direct application to wounds. An infusion of the bark has long been valued as a strong remedy for tapeworm.

Quinine *(Cinchona* spp.). Except under carefully controlled artificial conditions, these trees, native to the Andean highlands, cannot be grown in most climates. The flowers are rose, purple or pink, and the outer bark is white, gray-brown or golden brown. The inner bark of several species of *Cinchona* is the source of a number of alkaloids, the most important of which is quinine, well known as a highly effective—and for centuries the only—treatment for malaria.

Wild Rose (*Rosa* spp.). Wild roses of various species are spread over the Northern Hemisphere, and, by introduction, practically the entire world. The plant is typically a thorny shrub with white or pink flowers. The bright red fruits, or "hips," used for centuries in European folk medicine, are particularly effective against scurvy; we now know that this is due to the hips' rich concentration of vitamin C. Rose hips are still a major source of this important vitamin. Among many other uses to which various parts of wild roses have been put, a syrup made of rose petals and honey was frequently found effective against sore throat.

Meadow Saffron (*Colchicum autumnale*). Not to be confused with the saffron used as a spice (from a crocus), meadow saffron (also native to the Old World) is of the lily family. It is a perennial herb of somewhat unusual growth habits. The pale purple flowers with bright orange stamens appear alone on a white stalk in autumn. Not until the following spring do the leaves grow in and the fruits—brown capsules—ripen. The bulblike corms and the seeds are the source of colchicine, useful in treating gout and rheumatism, and now particularly valuable in genetic research for its property of affecting the division of cells.

Squill *(Urginea maritima)*. This species of squill, or sea onion, is a perennial herb with white or pink flowers, growing to about five feet. It is found in parts of Europe, Asia and Africa, particularly in the Mediterranean region. Squill contains numerous substances of medicinal value, including glycosides that act upon the heart. It is also used as a diuretic and as an expectorant in treating bronchitis. Dosage levels are critical; in large doses squill is extremely toxic, and in fact an extract of the plant is used as a rat poison! *(Poison.)*

Strychnine Tree (*Strychnos nux-vomica*). The famous poison, the alkaloid strychnine, is derived from the seeds of a number of vines, trees and shrubs of the genus *Strychnos*. The strychnine used for medical purposes usually comes from a southeast Asian tree also known as the nux-vomica tree. Growing to about forty feet, it has grayish brown bark and white flowers. The fruit, a greenish yellow when young, matures to a reddish yellow; the seeds, from which the alkaloid is derived, are gray. In measured doses, strychnine has a beneficially stimulating effect on the central nervous system and was formerly much used in treating certain cardiac and circulatory problems. It was once frequently also used as a gastrointestinal stimulant. (*Poison.*)

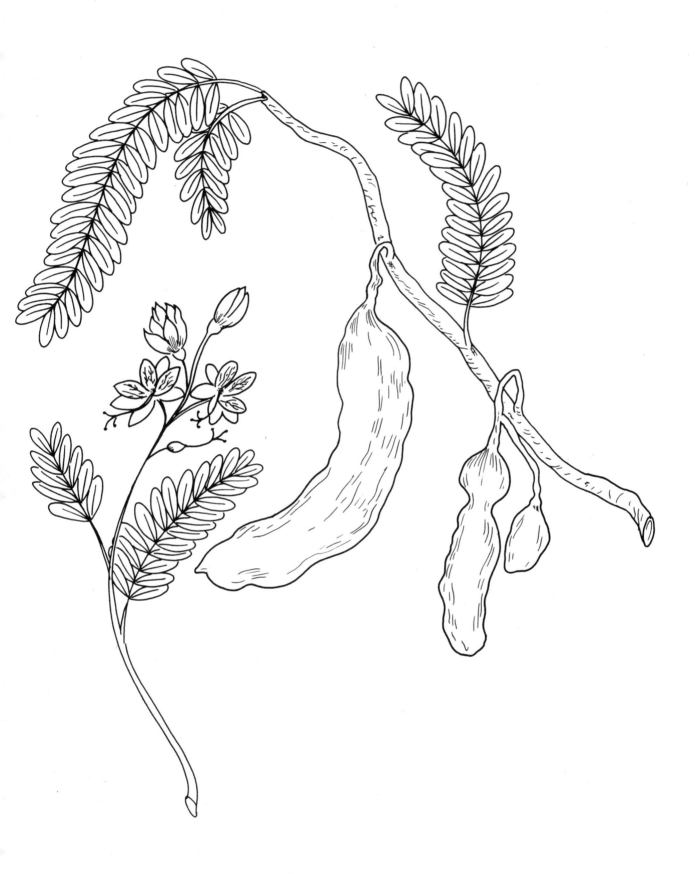

Tamarind *(Tamarindus indica)*. This handsome tree, growing to eighty feet, is a native of India, though widely cultivated in tropical regions throughout the world. Its bark is gray-brown, flowers yellow, veined in red, and fruit a cinnamon-colored pod. An important component of Indian cuisine, the crushed pulp of the fruit has also been widely used for various medicinal purposes, primarily as a laxative.

Milk Thistle *(Silybum marianum)*. Native to the Mediterranean region, the milk thistle has been naturalized in the United States and even grows as a weed in California. The leaves of this annual or biennial herb (growing to six feet) are veined with white and the flowers are purple. An extract of the seeds and roots has been used to treat the effects of drug and alcohol abuse, and is especially effective in ailments involving the liver.

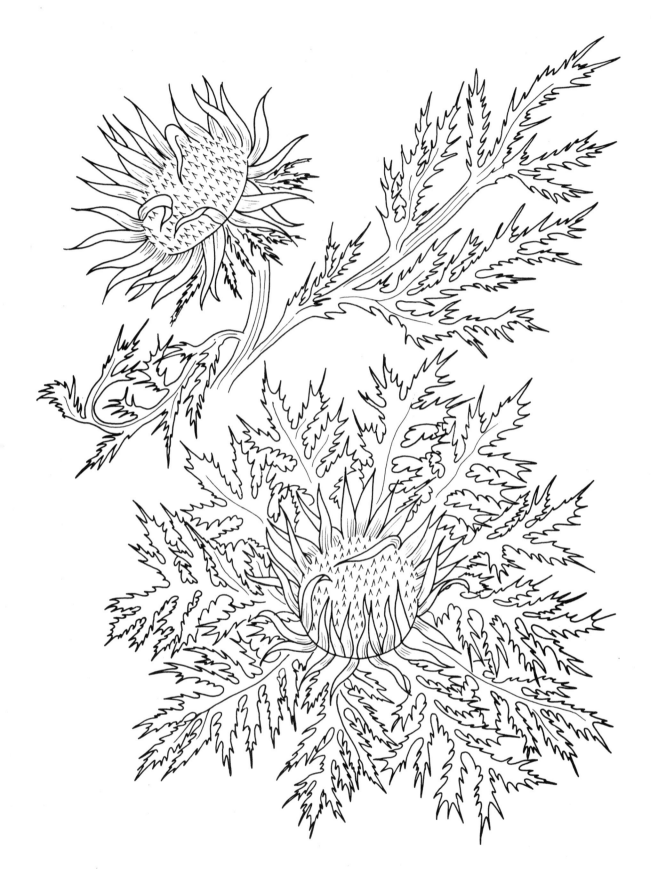

Stemless Thistle *(Carlina acaulis)*. This nine-inch-high perennial herb is native to Europe but naturalized in the United States. It is a composite with flowers formed by tiny brownish white disc florets surrounded by white bracts. Like many other thistles, the stemless thistle (so called from the fact that the flowers grow directly from the stalk or have at most very short stems) has medicinal value, yielding substances with antiseptic properties. Part of its value is legendary, however; this or a very similar thistle is said to have cured Charlemagne's army of the plague in the eighth century!

Valerian *(Valeriana officinalis)*. This perennial herb grows throughout much of Europe and Asia, sometimes reaching five feet. By introduction it has also spread throughout the midwestern and, particularly, the northeastern United States and parts of Canada. The flowers are white, pink or lavender. The dried rhizomes have been used for centuries as a drug. The active ingredients are a complex of substances known as valepotriates, which act directly on the central nervous system. Valerian acts as a sedative and tranquilizer in cases of insomnia, agitation and various nervous conditions. When used to treat fatigue, it acts as a stimulant. During World War I it was used to treat shell shock, and it has also been found of value as a treatment for heart and circulatory problems, as well as numerous other conditions.

Wild Yam (*Dioscorea villosa*). Hundreds of species of *Dioscorea* are found throughout the world, mostly in the tropics, and some provide important foods, the true yams, not the sweet potato called a "yam." The wild yam shown here is a vine growing to eighteen feet in the eastern and central United States. Its stems are reddish brown, flowers greenish. A tea made from the root was once used for rheumatism, gastrointestinal problems and morning sickness. Today many important drugs, especially steroid hormones, come from various yams. Contraceptives are made from yams, and yam derivatives are used to treat skin and allergic conditions, sexual disorders, rheumatoid arthritis and many other ailments. (May be mildly *poisonous*.)

Alphabetical List of Common Names

Alphabetical List of Scientific Names